The Calendar

A Year

by Patricia J. Murphy

Consulting Editor: Gail Saunders-Smith, PhD

Capstone *press*

Mankato, Minnesota

Pebble Books are published by Capstone Press,
151 Good Counsel Drive, P.O. Box 669, Mankato, Minnesota 56002.
www.capstonepress.com

1 2 3 4 5 6 10 09 08 07 06 05

Library of Congress Cataloging-in-Publication Data
Murphy, Patricia J., 1963–
    A year / by Patricia J. Murphy.
    p. cm.—(The calendar)
    Includes bibliographical references and index.
    ISBN 0-7368-3629-2 (hardcover)
    1. Year—Juvenile literature. I. Title.
CE13.M873 2005
529'.2—dc22
                                                    2004011903

Note to Parents and Teachers

The Calendar set supports national social studies and history
standards related to time, place, and change. This book describes
and illustrates a year. The images support early readers in
understanding the text. The repetition of words and phrases helps
early readers learn new words. This book also introduces early
readers to subject-specific vocabulary words, which are defined in
the Glossary section. Early readers may need assistance to read
some words and to use the Table of Contents, Glossary, Read More,
Internet Sites, and Index sections of the book.

Table of Contents

What Is a Year?. 5

Seasons 9

Once a Year. 13

End of the Year. 21

Glossary. 22

Read More 23

Internet Sites 23

Index 24

4

What Is a Year?

A year is 365 days long.
Each year begins
on January 1 and
ends on December 31.

The Calendar

January

Sunday	Monday	Tuesday	Wednesday	Thursday	Friday	Saturday
		1	2	3	4	5
6	7	8	9	10	11	12
13	14	15	16	17	18	19
20	21	22	23	24	25	26
27	28	29	30	31		

February

Sunday	Monday	Tuesday	Wednesday	Thursday	Friday	Saturday
					1	2
3	4	5	6	7	8	9
10	11	12	13	14	15	16
17	18	19	20	21	22	23
24	25	26	27	28		

March

Sunday	Monday	Tuesday	Wednesday	Thursday	Friday	Saturday
					1	2
3	4	5	6	7	8	9
10	11	12	13	14	15	16
17	18	19	20	21	22	23
24/31	25	26	27	28	29	30

April

Sunday	Monday	Tuesday	Wednesday	Thursday	Friday	Saturday
	1	2	3	4	5	6
7	8	9	10	11	12	13
14	15	16	17	18	19	20
21	22	23	24	25	26	27
28	29	30				

May

Sunday	Monday	Tuesday	Wednesday	Thursday	Friday	Saturday
			1	2	3	4
5	6	7	8	9	10	11
12	13	14	15	16	17	18
19	20	21	22	23	24	25
26	27	28	29	30	31	

June

Sunday	Monday	Tuesday	Wednesday	Thursday	Friday	Saturday
						1
2	3	4	5	6	7	8
9	10	11	12	13	14	15
16	17	18	19	20	21	22
23/30	24	25	26	27	28	29

July

Sunday	Monday	Tuesday	Wednesday	Thursday	Friday	Saturday
	1	2	3	4	5	6
7	8	9	10	11	12	13
14	15	16	17	18	19	20
21	22	23	24	25	26	27
28	29	30	31			

August

Sunday	Monday	Tuesday	Wednesday	Thursday	Friday	Saturday
				1	2	3
4	5	6	7	8	9	10
11	12	13	14	15	16	17
18	19	20	21	22	23	24
25	26	27	28	29	30	31

September

Sunday	Monday	Tuesday	Wednesday	Thursday	Friday	Saturday
1	2	3	4	5	6	7
8	9	10	11	12	13	14
15	16	17	18	19	20	21
22	23	24	25	26	27	28
29	30					

October

Sunday	Monday	Tuesday	Wednesday	Thursday	Friday	Saturday
		1	2	3	4	5
6	7	8	9	10	11	12
13	14	15	16	17	18	19
20	21	22	23	24	25	26
27	28	29	30	31		

November

Sunday	Monday	Tuesday	Wednesday	Thursday	Friday	Saturday
					1	2
3	4	5	6	7	8	9
10	11	12	13	14	15	16
17	18	19	20	21	22	23
24	25	26	27	28	29	30

December

Sunday	Monday	Tuesday	Wednesday	Thursday	Friday	Saturday
1	2	3	4	5	6	7
8	9	10	11	12	13	14
15	16	17	18	19	20	21
22	23	24	25	26	27	28
29	30	31				

The calendar shows
a year has 12 months.
Each month is about
four weeks long.

Seasons

A year has four seasons.
December, January,
and February are
winter months.
Spring comes in March,
April, and May.

June, July, and August
are summer months.
September, October,
and November make up
the fall.

Once a Year

Birthdays happen once a year. Ethan celebrates his birthday in January.

14

Holidays happen once a year. Valentine's Day is on February 14. Ethan makes cards for his friends.

Independence Day
is on July 4.
Ethan and his family
go on a picnic.

Thanksgiving is
in November.
Ethan helps his dad
bake pumpkin pies.

End of the Year

The year ends at midnight
on December 31.
Ethan's family has
a party. A new year
begins tomorrow.

Glossary

day—a period of time that equals 24 hours; there are seven days in each week.

calendar—a chart that shows all of the days, weeks, and months in a year; some calendars show one day, one week, or one month at a time.

celebrate—to do something fun on a special occasion; many people celebrate birthdays and holidays by having parties.

midnight—12:00 in the middle of the night; one day ends and another day begins at midnight.

month—one of the 12 parts that make up one year; each month is from 28 to 31 days long.

week—a period of seven days usually from Sunday to Saturday

Read More

Jordan, Denise. *Happy Birthday! Candle Time.* Chicago: Heinemann Library, 2002.

Kummer, Patricia K. *The Calendar.* Inventions that Shaped the World. New York: Franklin Watts, 2005.

Rockwell, Anne E. *Four Seasons Make a Year.* New York: Walker, 2004.

Internet Sites

FactHound offers a safe, fun way to find Internet sites related to this book. All of the sites on FactHound have been researched by our staff.

Here's how:

1. Visit *www.facthound.com*

2. Type in this special code **0736836292** for age-appropriate sites. Or enter a search word related to this book for a more general search.

3. Click on the **Fetch It** button.

FactHound will fetch the best sites for you!

Index

April, 9
August, 11
birthdays, 13
calendar, 7
days, 5
December, 5, 9, 21
February, 9, 15
holidays, 15, 17, 19, 21
January, 5, 9, 13
July, 11, 17

June, 11
March, 9
May, 9
midnight, 21
November, 11, 19
October, 11
seasons, 9, 11
September, 11
tomorrow, 21
weeks, 7

Word Count: 137
Grade: 1
Early-Intervention Level: 10

Editorial Credits

Sarah L. Schuette, editor; Jennifer Bergstrom, set designer

Photo Credits

All photographs by James Photography/James Menk except Corbis, 8 (top background); Digital Stock, 8 (bottom background); Photodisc, 10 (bottom background); Stockbyte, 10 (top background)